Maths Ar

Using Addition at Home

Tracey Steffora

www.raintreepublishers.co.uk
Visit our website to find out
more information about
Raintree books.

To order:

☎ Phone 0845 6044371

▤ Fax +44 (0) 1865 312263

▥ Email myorders@raintreepublishers.co.uk

Customers from outside the UK please telephone +44 1865 312262

Raintree is an imprint of Capstone Global Library Limited,
a company incorporated in England and Wales having its
registered office at 7 Pilgrim Street, London, EC4V 6LB
– Registered company number: 6695582

Edited by Rebecca Rissman, Tracey Steffora, and Catherine Veitch
Designed by Joanna Hinton-Malivoire
Picture research by Elizabeth Alexander
Production by Victoria Fitzgerald
Originated by Capstone Global Library Ltd
Printed and bound in China by Leo Paper Products Ltd

ISBN 978 1 406 22317 0 (hardback)
15 14 13 12 11
10 9 8 7 6 5 4 3 2 1

ISBN 978 1 406 22325 5 (paperback)
16 15 14 13 12
10 9 8 7 6 5 4 3 2 1

British Library Cataloguing in Publication Data
Steffora, Tracey.
Using addition at home. -- (Maths around us)
513.2'11-dc22

Acknowledgements
The author and publisher are grateful to the following for
permission to reproduce photographs: Alamy pp. 4 top left (©
Photo Network), 4 bottom right (© Randy Romano), 5 top right
(© Jon Arnold Images Ltd), 5 bottom left (© Barry Lewis), 14 (©
ImagesBazaar); Corbis pp. 6 (© Inmagine Asia), 10 (© Bloomimage);
Getty Images pp. 15, 23 glossary – text (Jam Photography);
Photolibrary pp. 4 bottom left (Quentin Bargate/Loop Images), 7 (I
Love Images), 11 (Jon Feingersh/Blend Images), 19, 23 glossary – email
(Radius Images); Shutterstock pp. 4 top right (© mahout), 5 top left
(© wavebreakmedia ltd.), 5 bottom right (© Dmitriy Shironosov), 18
(© wavebreakmedia ltd.), 22 (© Vasina Natalia).

Cover photograph of a family preparing a meal reproduced with
permission of Shutterstock (© wavebreakmedia ltd.). Back cover
photograph of a girl knocking on a front door reproduced with
permission of Photolibrary (I Love Images).

We would like to thank Nancy Harris, Dee Reid, and Diana Bentley for
their assistance in the preparation of this book.

Every effort has been made to contact copyright holders of
material reproduced in this book. Any omissions will be rectified in
subsequent printings if notice is given to the publisher.

Contents

Around the world

People live in homes.

At home we share meals with family and friends.

One more

Four people are sharing a meal.

There is a knock at the door.

It is a friend!

start with

add

How many people are there in total?

$$4 + 1 = 5$$

Four plus one equals five.

There are five people in total.

Two more

Four people are sharing a meal.

The phone rings.

Grandma and Grandad are coming over!

start with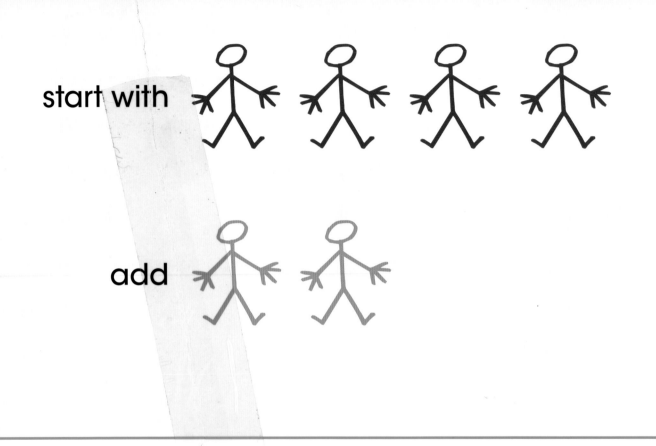

add

How many people are there in total?

$$4 + 2 = 6$$

Four plus two equals six.

There are six people in total.

Three more

Four people are sharing a meal.

They get a text.

Three friends are coming over!

start with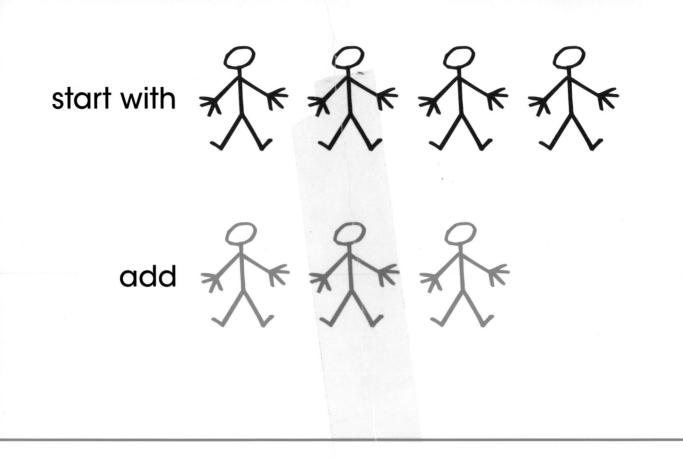

add

How many people are there in total?

$$4 + 3 = 7$$

Four plus three equals seven.

There are seven people in total.

Four more

Four people are making a meal.

They get an email.

Four more people are coming over!

start with

add

How many people are there in total?

$$4 + 4 = 8$$

Four plus four equals eight.

There are eight people in total.

Clean up

Sharing a meal is fun. But there is lots of washing-up to do afterwards.

Picture glossary

email message sent or received through a computer. It is called electronic mail.

text message sent or received through a mobile phone

Index

Notes for parents and teachers
Before reading
Discuss with children different activities that occur at home. They might mention having meals, playing with toys, washing-up, etc. Encourage them to describe what happens during each activity and then review and highlight any language or description that implies addition (e.g. putting forks and spoons on the table). Remind them that they use addition every day, even when they are not aware of it.

After reading
To help give children a concrete sense of addition, you might have them act out some of the addition stories in this text. For example, four children could be sitting at a table, and then another child knocks on the door. Review how they can tell this story using numbers and symbols (4+1=5). Encourage them to create their own scenarios with different quantities of children and record their stories with words, drawings and/or equations.